Expressive Kayaking

(Kayak Line Dancing)

Leslie Dunn

Cover photo by Captain Paul Eidman

DEDICATION

To Elaine Mravetz whose elegance, passion and dedication
to Freestyle Canoeing inspired me to create this
new and fun thing to do with our kayaks.

CONTENTS

ACKNOWLEDGMENTS

Thank you, Lee.
Without you this book would not be possible
.

Chapter One
What is Expressive Kayaking?

In 2001, while kayaking with paddling buds in North Central Florida, one of the men whispered, "Look at Laurel."

I looked at her maneuvering her twelve foot kayak around a hairpin turn and then looked back at him with a question in my eyes. You know the look – "Huh?"

Again whispering, he said, "She's beautiful."

I looked again at Laurel. The question went verbal: "Huh?"

"Look at the way she handles her kayak. Perfect control…sexy."

The guy I'm talking to is married, as is Laurel, and in our world we don't cross the line. Yet, her expertise captivated him and he responded in a way that men do when something tugs at their, ummm, heart. Trying to see her through his eyes, again I looked at her.

I didn't get the 'sexy' part but as she paddled with confident, powerful and deliberate strokes I thought, "Kayaking is beautiful."

Jump forward fourteen years. Lee and I are at a Boy Scout camp in Ohio where I'm getting tested to recertify as a kayak instructor with the American Canoe Association (ACA). During this same weekend, ACA is hosting a Freestyle Canoeing competition. Freestyle Canoeists maintain perfect control of their boats while performing a variety of strokes to music.

At the registration table sits Elayne Mravetz. She projects warmth and confidence, a pixie of a woman with a smile bigger than she is. Elayne's a Freestyle Canoe pro and watching her perform is like watching a ballerina. She wears her canoe like a tutu; the oar, her slippers. Her movements are as fluid as the water surrounding her as she zens with her canoe. Sunshine reflects on her toned arms and brightens her smile. She is lost in the music and controls her canoe with such mastery that watching her makes me weep.

If my Florida paddle bud could see her he might, just for the duration of Elayne's performance, reconsider crossing the line.

After John, my ACA instructor, said I was good to go, Lee and I hung out while I dried from the flip John had me perform. Stress about recertifying no longer preoccupied me and I relaxed watching other canoeists compete against Elayne. The music, their touching dedications to loved ones, the strength and sureness of their oar placement...

Click We move our kayaks with beauty and grace. We maintain control. Most of the time.

Click Why don't *we* do what these canoeists are doing?

Double click We *can* do what they're doing.

Press *Enter.*

Back home I set up music and set out in my kayak. The song I chose is, "*Cetan Lutah (Red-Tail Hawk)*" from the album, *"Animal Totems,"* written and performed by Arvel Bird, a Native American. It's the most beautiful song I've ever heard.

Imitating the canoeists I push my limits with deep bow sweeps, reverse stern sweeps, strong forward strokes and pivots. But something's missing. My repertoire is too limited.

Forget solo. Get other paddlers involved. Like line dancing, we can create formations and synchronize movements to music but we can do it with even more expression. Because we float.

Benefits of
Expressive Kayaking

A few years ago after surgery, I decided to rehabilitate myself through walking. Three to four days a week I trudged for miles. Bored and discouraged, my commitment to my self-imposed therapy plunged. I created a playlist of alternating slow and fast songs. The mixture worked. I power walked to the fast songs and slowed my tempo to the others. The music distracted me from what truly was exercise.

The point is, Expressive Kayaking works the same magic. Kayaking to music takes "work" out of workout and is a fun way to get fit with friends. Any form of kayaking – river, sea, lake, ocean – is a stress buster but allowing music to guide your strokes immerses you to whole new level. The first couple times I did it, I didn't realize how much energy I expended until I brought in my boat, caught my breath and headed for a shower.

The requirements are as few as three experienced kayakers, quiet water and music.

One of the things I tell my students is that almost anyone can kayak – men, women, young, old - it is the "equal opportunity" of sports. As the fastest growing sport in America, it's applications expand. Over the past ten years kayak fishing and Stand Up Paddleboarding have exploded. And now, Expressive Kayaking. If you have good boat control, you're ahead of the game. If you don't, try some Expressive Kayaking and you will achieve it. Note: You must have experience kayaking first. This is not something a complete newbie should try.

How to Get Started

Most recreational kayakers are noncompetitive. We are more about enjoying the scenery than whitewater paddlers. Expressive Kayaking as a group is all about cooperation.

To begin, start the group without music practising basic strokes in unison encouraging everyone to match one another's style. Cover the basics – forward, reverse, pivoting, etc. If someone isn't doing a stroke the right way, they'll need to be brought up to speed to keep the group aligned. For example, rotate from your waist doing a pivot. If someone turns only their head while reaching back with their paddle, and doesn't rotate their torso, they'll need to learn the right way to do it.

After everyone matches stroke styles, it's time to learn formations. You might want to remove pages of this book and insert them into plastic sleeves for quick reference while practicing on the water.

After your group memorizes several formations, it's time to turn on the music. Expressive Kayaking works best with slow songs. I imagine doing it to the accompaniment of a drum circle with lights on the kayaks would be a memorable event as a participant and observer.

Kayaks sit low in the water making it difficult for spectators to see formations. An easy fix is doing Expressive Kayaking at an infrequently used boat ramp on a lake if you are fortunate enough to live near one. It's not impossible to do it on slow rivers but when holding a static formation be prepared to drift. The gentle current, though, enhances formations like "Star," which can be graduated through movement to explode.

Chapter Two illustrates formations using the theme, "Native American." Some are static requiring only that paddlers get into the correct spot (Star), some require gentle movement (Snake) and others will make you sweat (Warrior). You'll find formations for as few as three kayaks up to groups of eight.

Chapter Three illustrates a sample routine that requires movement. In rhythm with the music, kayaks flow like a waterfall or simulate an eagle in flight.

Chapter Four reviews how to perform strokes.

I'd love to hear about your Expressive Kayaking. Pictures, links to videos on YouTube – please email them to KayakLessons@yahoo.com. Send your location and I'll add it to an interactive map. No doubt, your ideas will generate a spark in someone else's imagination. Express yourself!

Leslie Dunn
Author
ACA Certified Kayak Instructor
ACA Adaptive Paddling Endorsement

Chapter Two
FORMATIONS

This chapter introduces the names and strokes of basic formations I've created based on Native American objects and symbols.

For best maneuverability, do Expressive Kayaking using boats no longer than 10 feet. When analyzing and reproducing formations, please notice the location of the bow and stern in the pictures.

Bow

Stern

In the illustrations, I apologize that boats are of different widths and lengths. Please forgive the limits of my abilities with Microsoft Word. When actually performing the formations, all boats must be of the same length for uniformity.

Sidewinder

(Any number of kayaks)
Side Draw stroke
(For a more elegant variation, do the
Sculling Draw stroke.)

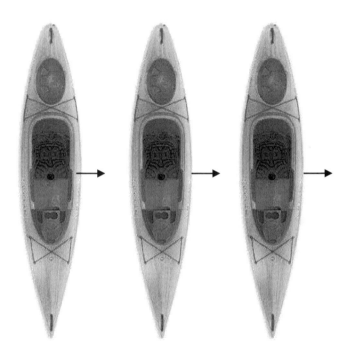

Rattlesnake

(Minimum three kayaks)

Odd numbered kayaks paddle gently on left to maintain boat pointing to the right; even number kayaks paddle gently on right. Odd and even boats reverse paddling sides to generate movements of a Snake.

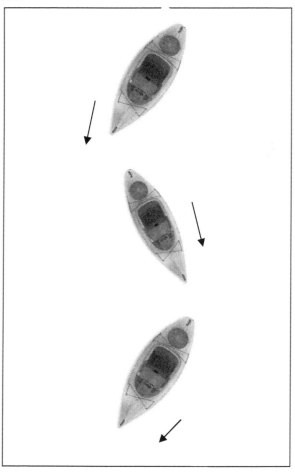

Warrior

(Any number of kayaks)
Deep, deliberate forward strokes in unison.
Think: soldiers marching.

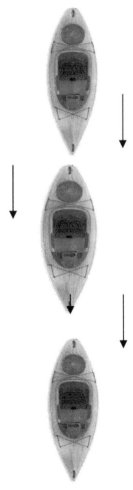

Pivot

(Any number of kayaks – shown with two)

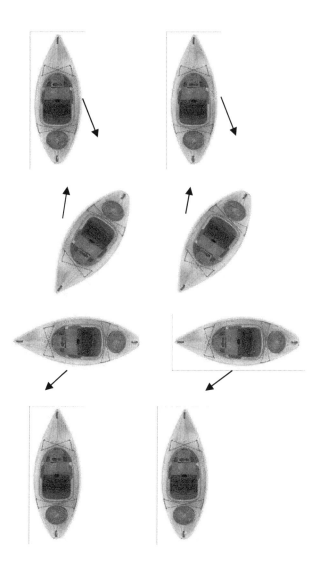

<u>Daisy</u>
(Minimum four kayaks)

- Paddlers direct their bow toward each other

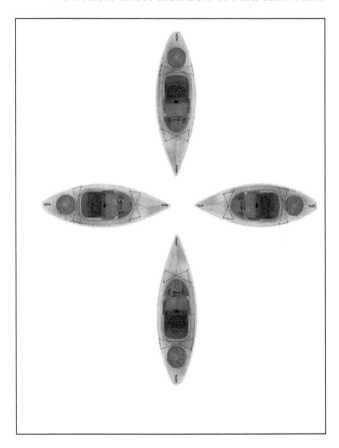

Star

(Minimum four kayaks)

- Paddlers direct their sterns toward each other
- To twirl the star, each paddler performs sculling draw strokes.

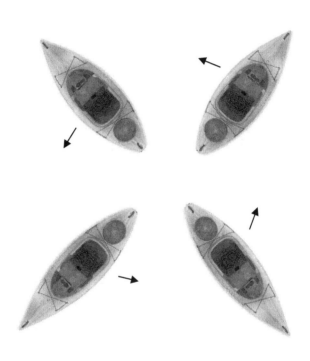

Moon

(Minimum four kayaks)
- Tight or wide circle

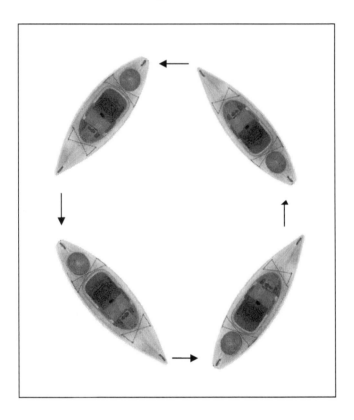

Cross
(Minimum four kayaks)

At first glance this formation appears identical to Daisy but notice different placement of bows and sterns. Heavier weighted sterns hold the cross "arm" in place.

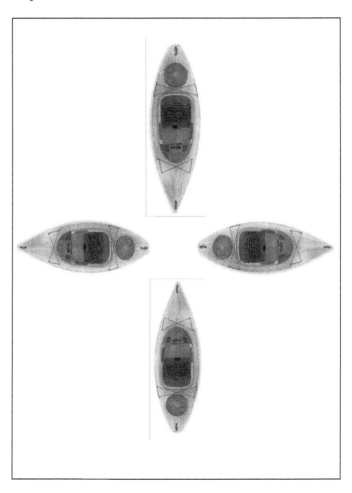

Tomahawk
(Minimum four kayaks)

Eagle
(Five kayaks)

Sun

(Minimum five kayaks)

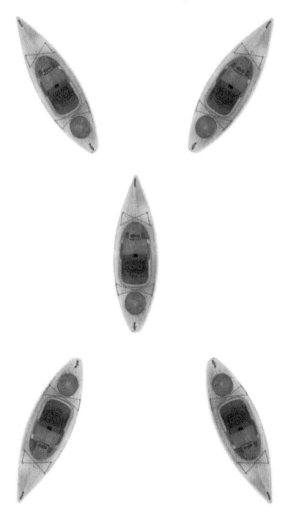

Fire

(Minimum five kayaks)

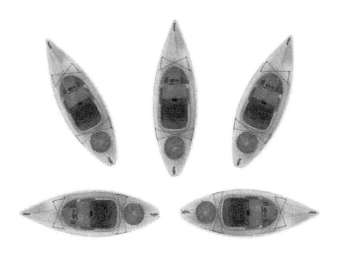

Easily expand fire using more kayaks as flames and more horizontal kayaks to lengthen logs.

Teepee

(Minimum five – with seven, form the floor of the teepee)

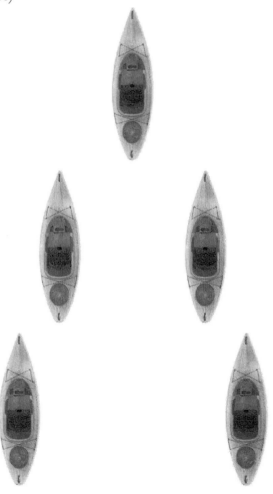

Arrow
(Minimum six kayaks)

Arrowhead

(Minimum six kayaks in tight formation)

Human
(Six kayaks)

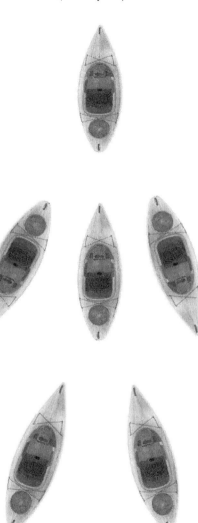

Dream Catcher

(Minimum seven kayaks. With thirteen kayaks, create a large circle using five on top, a smaller circle beneath it with three and five hanging from the bottom of each circle as the feathers.)

Bear Paw

Paddlers who are the toes — extend your blade in front of your boat for the claw.

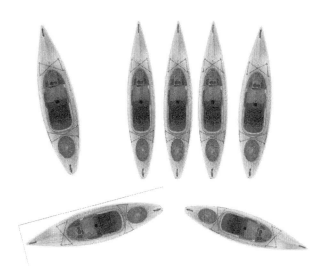

Indian Headgear

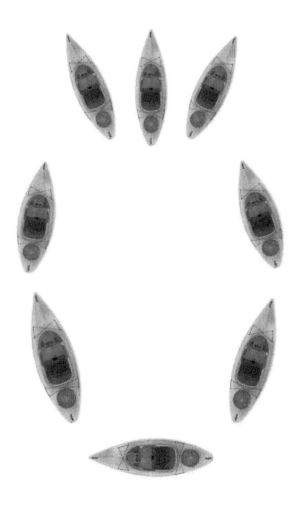

Chapter Two
Movement Formations

In this section you'll find formations that require movement.

Waterfall

(Minimum six kayaks)

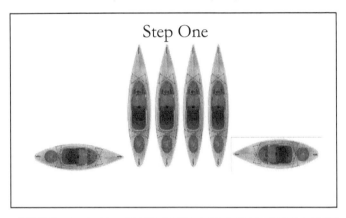

Step One

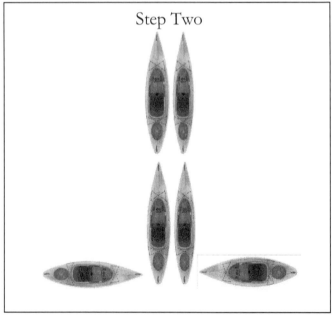

Step Two

Step Three

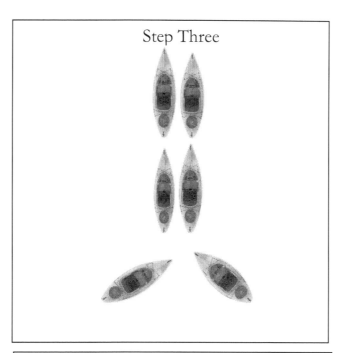

Step Four

Step Five

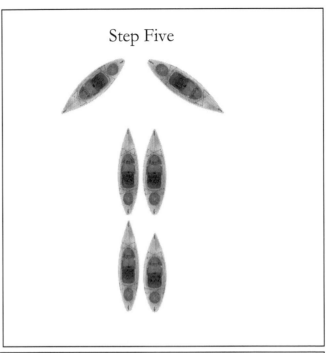

Step Six

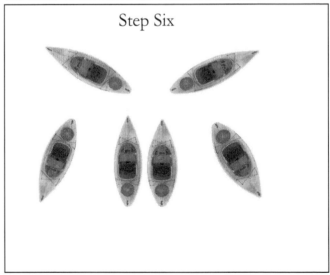

Step Seven

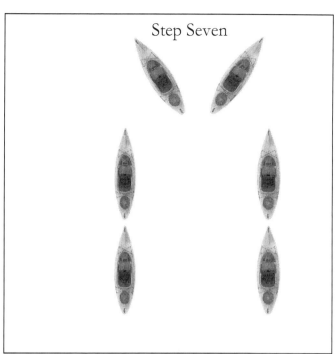

Step Eight

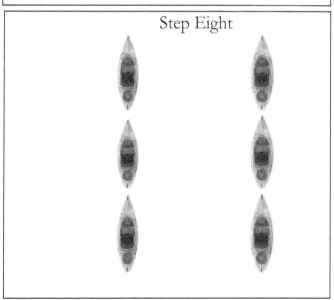

Flying Eagle
Step One
Form a tail if three more kayaks are available.

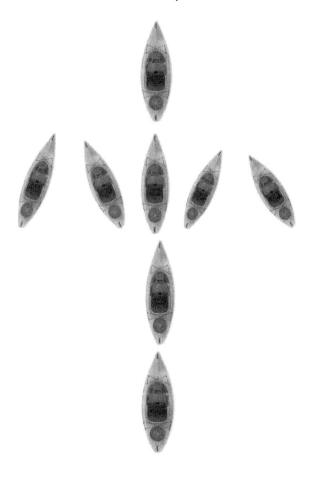

Step Two
Just the wings move

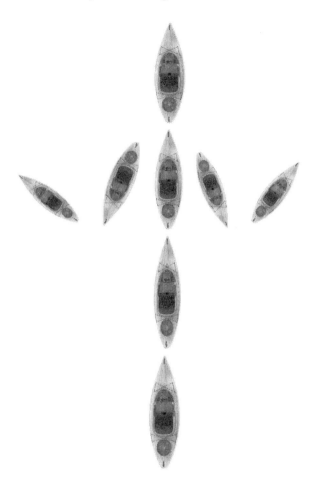

Step Three

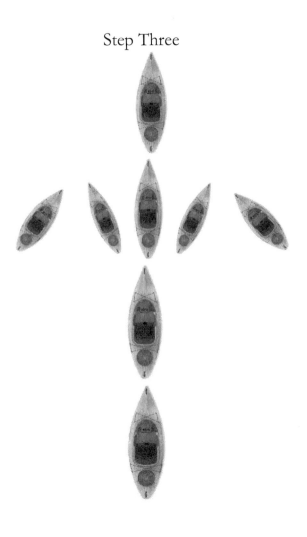

Step Four

Fish Swimming

Step One

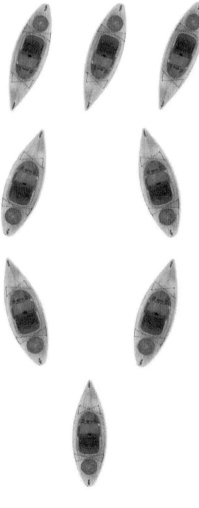

Step Two

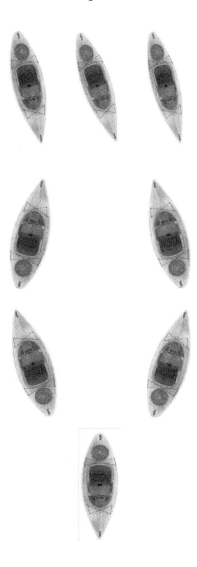

Chapter Three
Sample Routine

The music and theme you choose determines formations your group uses for Expressive kayaking. Boat lengths also are a determining factor. Pivots, for example, in an eight foot boat take only two strokes but in a ten foot boat take three or four strokes.

As noted previously, my examples are based on the theme, Native Americans. Create your own themes. Here's a couple ideas: Different types of fish – octopus, starfish, dolphin, conch. Or sky objects – airplane, sun, star, moon, comet.

Your group may consider purchasing Swim Paddles for your hands. Use them for gentle movements or formations that require boats to stay close to each other. Don't get Swim Paddles that are like gloves.

Get the ones with straps you can easily slip on and off your hand.

Next, you'll find a sample routine that transitions kayaks from one formation to another.

Before the music starts, paddlers get out into the water and line up next to one another like this:

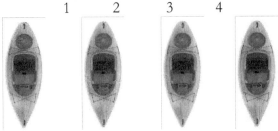

Leave enough room between the boats so each kayaker can paddle. Boats one and three do three forward strokes.

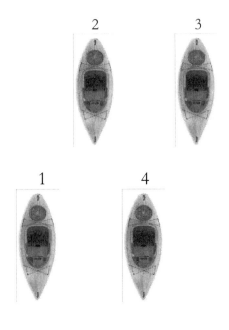

Now, everyone pivot in place which reverses each boat's bow and stern.

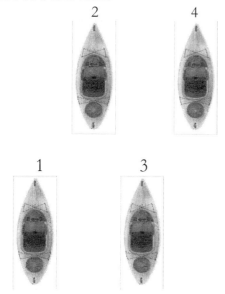

Next, transition to the Daisy formation. Here's how:

Boat 1: Half pivot

Boat 1 does a half pivot such that the bow of the boat faces the middle of the group.

Boat 2: Full pivot:
Boat 2 does a full pivot so that their bow points toward the middle of the group

Boat 3: Sculling draw stroke
Simultaneously, boat 3 draws their boat sideways with a couple sculling draw strokes to line up bow with boat 2.

Boat 4: Half pivot
Boat 4 does a half pivot.

With these strokes, the group forms a Daisy.

Most songs last three to four minutes. If the song ends with a gentle beat, doing draw strokes sets the Daisy spinning.

Now it's your turn. Get your group, practice matching each other's paddle strokes, move on to formations, put on the music and have fun!

Chapter Four
Review of Strokes

Forward Stroke: There are three parts – the catch, propulsion and exit. Be sure to rotate your torso with the catch for every stroke. The correct placement is the blade catching the water at your feet and exiting at your seat. Submerge the blade during propulsion and slice it out of the water when it reaches your seat.

Tip: To make the bow turn to the right, do a forward stroke on the left. To make the bow go left, forward stroke on the right.

Back Stroke: Rotate your torso from shoulder to belly button as one unit - do not turn your head independently. Pretend your neck is inflexible and follows the direction of your shoulders. You should literally be able to see what's behind you. If you've developed a habit of turning your head only when you backstroke, sit on the ground and, without a paddle in your hands, rotate from your torso. Also, for an effective back stroke, reach the blade f-a-r behind the seat. Doing strokes half way works but not very well. To move your boat, utilize the blade as effectively as possible.

Side Draw: Keeping your hips stationary, twist from belly button up toward the side on which you'll perform the draw. If you want to go sideways to the right, twist toward the right; to the left if you want to move sideways to the left.

Place the tip of the blade on the surface of the water almost as far as you can reach. Caution to male readers: When you place the tip of the blade out as far as you can reach, if you power into the side draw you will flip so there are two choices: Put the tip of the blade as far as you can reach but don't give it everything you've got *or* keep your elbow slightly flexed, not fully extended, when placing the tip of the blade on the water.

Your lower hand will be near the water on the paddle shaft and the upper hand chest high holding the shaft of the paddle. With the lower hand pull the paddle toward you and, *at the same time*, push forward away from the kayak with your upper hand. It's a simultaneous push and pull. When pushing with your upper hand, don't let it raise over your head. It takes some muscle to keep it chest high. (When performing strokes, anytime your hand is over your head, your arms are out of the "*paddler's box" and you lose strength.) The correct position at the end of the stroke is "looking at your watch" on the wrist of your upper hand. At this point, your blade should be vertical – straight up and down – and your boat moved to the side on which you performed the draw.

Tip: Stop when the blade is about six inches from the boat to stop it going under the boat which will make you flip.

Raise the blade slightly with your lower hand while rotating your fist so your knuckles face the bow. This puts the blade into the slice position. Don't pull the blade completely out of the water. While dragging the blade up, rotate your wrist with knuckles facing the sky which puts the blade into position for the next draw stroke.

*Paddlers Box: While sitting, with your hands draw an imaginary line from both shoulders to your knees. Draw another line from there down to your knees. That is the Paddler's Box. Whitewater folks can let their hands drift over their head for strokes because they don't have as much boat to move as recreational paddlers. By staying in the box, we achieve more muscle power to move our larger and heavier kayaks.

Sculling Draw: Turn your torso toward the side you want to draw. Extend your blade and put the tip to the water but not as far out as the extension for the draw stroke. (Please see warning to male paddlers in description of Draw stroke.) What you are going to do is pretend you are spreading peanut butter on a piece of bread – your paddle is the butter knife and water is the peanut butter. Remember to keep your upper arm no more than chest high.

Start slicing the blade back and forth in a figure eight by rotating your knuckles in each direction, never letting the blade completely out of the water.

Each boat has a side draw sweet spot. On my Pungo, if I draw stroke behind the seat and just in front of the bulkhead my boat moves with precision meaning the bow and stern move sideways at the same time. If I draw stroke at any other spot, either the bow or stern move independently. Test your boat to find the right spot to move the boat so that both bow and stern move together.

ABOUT THE AUTHOR

Leslie Dunn started writing at age fourteen, kayaking in 2001 and teaching kayak lessons in 2009. She published, "Quiet Water Kayaking – A Beginner's Guide," and "Rudolf Virchow – Four Lives in One." She lives in Tennessee.

19386674R00033

Printed in Great Britain
by Amazon